Walter
Cronkite This is
Walter Cronkite

Walter Cronkite

This is
Walter Cronkite

by Paula Taylor / Norita Larson
illustrated by Harold Henriksen

Creative Education
Mankato, Minnesota 56001

Published by Creative Educational Society, Inc., 123 South Broad Street. Mankato. Minnesota 56001.
Copyright © 1975 by Creative Educational Society, Inc. International copyrights reserved in all countries.
No part of this book may be reproduced in any form without written permission from the publisher.
Printed in the United States.
Distributed by Childrens Press, 1224 West Van Buren Street, Chicago, Illinois 60607.

Library of Congress Number: 75-2103   ISBN: 0-87191-424-7

Library of Congress Cataloging in Publication Data
Larson, Norita.   This is Walter Cronkite.
SUMMARY: A brief biography of a CBS newsman, anchorman for television's
longest-running news show.
1. Cronkite, Walter—Juvenile literature. (1. Cronkite, Walter,   2. Television
broadcasting of news—Biography) I. Taylor, Paula, joint author.
II. Henriksen, Harold, ill.   III. Title.
PN4874.C84L3   070.4'092'4 (B) (92) 75-2103
ISBN 0-87191-424-7

INTRODUCTION

As anchorman for television's longest-running and most successful evening news show, Walter Cronkite has become a familiar figure to millions of Americans. They depend on him to tell them what's happening in the world.

As managing editor of CBS television's news, Walter Cronkite is the one who decides what will appear on the "electronic front page." He has tremendous power to shape the news. But Cronkite is careful not to abuse this power. He insists on being strictly objective in reporting the news. He tries to air all sides of every issue and refuses to mingle his own opinions with the facts.

Walter Cronkite is well-qualified for his important job. He has been a newsman for over 30 years. Although he never finished college, he has received many honorary degrees and awards. More than any other newsman, Walter Cronkite has helped set today's high standards for television news.

Walter Cronkite

This is
Walter Cronkite

By late afternoon, the CBS television newsroom is in a state of feverish activity. Teletype machines and typewriters clatter away, keeping pace with fast-breaking stories around the world. Film and copy editors look rushed and tense. The deadline for the evening news is fast approaching.

About 5:00 p.m. Walter Cronkite emerges from his small, cluttered office and strides through the newsroom to his anchor desk. He's carrying a copy of the script he's just finished writing. He looks over the latest wire service bulletins to make sure nothing has been missed. It's up to him to make the final decision on what stories will go out over the air. He leans over to question a writer about a film segment. Then he scribbles a correction in the margin of his script. Finally, he reads the completed script aloud, timing it with a stopwatch.

Producer Leslie Midgeley motions Cronkite into his office. CBS in Rome has just obtained an exclusive interview. It's being sent via satellite to New York. Cronkite joins a group of staff members in the producer's office to look over the film and decide whether to include it on the evening news.

No lineup of stories is completely fixed until Walter

Cronkite signs off the air. If a big story breaks while he's on the air, an editor will hand him the teletype transcript through a slot under the desk. Then it's up to Cronkite to make the split-second decision how to fit the story in.

Watching Walter Cronkite during the last few minutes before he goes on the air is almost like watching an Apollo countdown.

6:13 p.m. Television cameras are being set up. Lights are turned on Cronkite and on the map behind him. Walter pulls on his suit jacket and straightens his tie.

6:20 p.m. The news staff continues to work feverishly. The copy editor thumbs nervously through stories still coming from writers. Walter Cronkite is the only one who appears calm. But he clears his throat several times. He worries about losing his voice.

6:25 p.m. "FIVE MINUTES!" someone calls. Cronkite looks over his script one last time.

6:27 p.m. Walter reaches for the small microphone lying on his desk. THREE MINUTES! He attaches the mike to his shirt.

6:28 p.m. TWO MINUTES! Resignedly, Cronkite lets a make-up man touch up his face.

6:29 p.m. ONE MINUTE! A late bulletin on a murder in Boston has just come over the teletype. Should it be included in tonight's news? "No," says Cronkite. He runs a comb through his hair. With seconds to go, he whirls around to face the cameras.

The ON THE AIR sign flashes; and Cronkite begins,

"Good evening." The next half hour is perfectly timed and co-ordinated. The cameras shift smoothly from Cronkite to the film segments, then back to the anchorman. Finally, right on schedule, he signs off with the words familiar to millions of Americans: "That's the way it is. This is Walter Cronkite for CBS News. Good night."

The lights are turned off, and the cameras are wheeled away. Walter Cronkite looks weary, but he's not finished yet. Many stations carry the CBS Evening News live. But others delay broadcast and show it at 7:00 p.m., Eastern Standard Time. So Walter Cronkite and his staff stand by to correct any mistakes or to include late-breaking news.

Today the tape is fine. Most of Cronkite's newscasts are. He's a professional. He's been in the news business for over 30 years. But he didn't intend to become a television anchorman. In fact, he got into television newscasting almost by accident.

Cronkite grew up in Kansas City, Missouri, and Houston, Texas. Life was comfortable, but not exciting enough to suit young Walter. His father was a dentist, but Walter dreamed of having a more daring and adventurous career.

In high school, he briefly considered becoming a mining engineer, but gave up this idea when he had difficulty with chemistry and physics. He liked baseball and football, but wasn't good enough to make the high school teams. He was more successful at writing stories for the school newspaper and yearbook than at either science or sports.

When he finished high school, Walter entered the Uni-

versity of Texas to study economics and political science. He helped pay his tuition by working as a reporter covering the Texas State Legislature and as a radio announcer. Soon he was spending more time at the capitol than in class. He found reporting on the work of real politicians much more interesting than studying political science in school. In his junior year, Walter quit the university to become a full-time reporter with the *Houston Press*.

A year later, he took a job as a radio sports announcer in Kansas City. At that time, instead of covering games live, stations often faked broadcasts of football games from the wire-service play-by-play reports. This is what Walter was told to do.

Although he was somewhat uneasy about it, he did the job with characteristic thoroughness. He got the colleges to send him photographs of their stadiums, the names and numbers of their players, recordings by their bands, and their plans for card stunts. He even telephoned local people who were planning to attend the games to find out what they would be wearing. "Why there's Doctor John Smith in his new brown checked coat," he would shout excitedly over a recording of crowd noise. "How d'ya like the game so far, Doc?"

Walter Cronkite's sportscasts were so realistic that his audience sometimes didn't know the reports of the games were faked. The broadcasts were popular with Kansas City sports fans but not with the Federal Communications Commission. Station KCMO was given a reprimand, and Walter's assignment was changed. He began covering actual games from a real press box.

But even then, Cronkite felt there was too much show business in radio. Besides, he had met a spirited red-head named Mary Elizabeth Maxwell, who was women's editor for the *Kansas City Journal*. Betsy urged him to go back to newspaper reporting. She had heard there was a job available with the United Press. Walter applied and got the job. When his pay was raised to $35 a week, he and Betsy were married.

Shortly afterwards, Walter was sent to El Paso, Texas, to set up a new United Press Bureau there. He covered stories in Dallas, Austin, and Houston. The Cronkites' life settled into a comfortable routine. Then, on December 7, 1941, the Japanese attacked Pearl Harbor. The United States entered World War II, and Walter was sent overseas as a United Press correspondent.

First he covered the battle of the Atlantic and the U.S. landings in North Africa. Then he was assigned to cover the air war out of London. It was a dangerous job. To get eyewitness accounts of the action, correspondents went along on bombing raids. Many never came back.

During one bombing run over Germany the fighting was so fierce that Cronkite manned a machine gun along with the crew. While tracer bullets burned and gunfire crackled, Walter watched German and American planes burst into flames and go down. When he returned to London, he found that 13 out of 67 American planes had been lost. One of his friends, a fellow reporter, had been killed.

Among the press corps, Cronkite became known for his courage under fire. But Walter himself is modest about his war-time bravery. "I was very brave," he says, "only because I did everything only once, before I really knew how hard it was. I'm a real nut. I'll try anything once."

Cronkite also may have decided the exciting eyewitness reports he was getting were worth the risks he had to take. His stories had begun appearing under his name in such well-known newspapers as the *New York Times*.

Cronkite got the chance to cover a very big story almost

by accident. On the night of June 5, 1944, he was just going to bed when an Air Force officer knocked on his door. "There's a pretty good story breaking," he said. "I think you'd better come with us."

As they got into a waiting car, the officer explained that the long-awaited invasion of Europe was starting. A B-17 bomber group was to fly over the coast at low altitude to spearhead the attack. "We can take only one correspondent," the officer added apologetically. "We drew lots and you won."

At dawn, Cronkite was flying over the French coast, watching Allied troops pour onto the Normandy beaches. It was a thrilling moment.

A few months after D-day, he got even closer to the action. Paratroopers of the 101st Airborne Division were making a glider drop in Holland behind German lines. Cronkite volunteered to go along.

On the morning of September 17, he crawled into a glider carrying 14 soldiers and their equipment. As the glider was jerked into the air by a tow plane, it began to shake violently. Cronkite, who had never been in a glider before, was sure it was being torn apart. He was even more alarmed when, after being cut loose from the tow plane, the glider went into a nose dive. (No one had bothered to tell him that this was the safest way for the pilot to avoid anti-aircraft fire.)

To give the soldiers a chance to scatter quickly and avoid enemy fire, the pilot made a crash landing in a potato field. The men tumbled out. Helmets flew in all directions. Cronkite grabbed the first helmet he saw and clapped it on his head.

Although he had no idea where he was going, he started

WAR CORRESPONDENT
1946

crawling across the field. Looking back over his shoulder, he noticed a dozen other men crawling along behind him. He dropped into a ditch. They followed. "Are you sure we're going in the right direction, Major?" one of the men asked. For a moment, Cronkite was puzzled. Then he took off his helmet and stared at the insignia. Sure enough — he'd grabbed the wrong one.

There were other mix-ups. With the Germans in retreat, Walter Cronkite was put in charge of setting up United Press operations in Belgium and the Netherlands. Occasionally he arrived in towns ahead of the Canadian troops who were supposed to free them. The townspeople, thinking Cronkite was a high-ranking officer of the liberating army, welcomed him with flowers and grateful speeches. When the weary Canadian soldiers finally arrived, they found a newsman had

16

stolen the show. "They were not amused," Cronkite recalls with a chuckle.

Although he was only 29 years old when the war ended, Walter Cronkite had become an experienced and highly-respected reporter. He was put in charge of the United Press Bureaus in Holland, Belgium, and Luxembourg. Then he was assigned to cover the Nuremberg trials of German leaders accused of war crimes.

In 1946, Cronkite was sent to Moscow as U.P.'s chief Russian correspondent. For two years he covered the beginnings of the Cold War from the other side of the Iron Curtain. It was a frustrating assignment. Travel was limited to a small area around Moscow. Foreign reporters were forbidden to interview any Russian citizens, including government officials. Since they were not able to do any "live" reporting, correspondents were forced to rely on the official Soviet press for information. Cronkite and the other reporters often filed stories which merely repeated Soviet newspaper articles word for word. But even then, their stories were often censored without explanation.

The Soviet government was trying to keep all foreigners from mixing with the Russian people. Diplomats and reporters from the Western countries were treated harshly and with suspicion. Sometimes they were even arrested.

Cronkite knew all this, but he was not really alarmed until an Associated Press correspondent who was a good friend of his was accused of being a spy. As evidence of his guilt, the Russian government produced a story the reporter had written on Soviet air transport. The information for the article had come from the official Soviet press. Any of the correspondents could have written it.

Cronkite's friend was forced to leave the Soviet Union within 48 hours. Walter drove him to the airport. As they said goodby, Cronkite wondered which of the correspondents would be arrested next.

When the United Press asked him to return to the United States in 1948, Cronkite was happy to do so. For the first time in seven years, he and Betsy were able to enjoy a normal family life.

Shortly after his return, Cronkite was offered a job reporting Washington news for a group of Midwestern radio stations. He had some doubts about going back into radio broadcasting. He still felt that only newspapers presented serious news; radio news was more like show business. But the salary was twice what he was making as a United Press reporter. He took the job.

A year later, Cronkite joined CBS as a member of the network's radio news staff in Washington. When the Korean War broke out, he was asked to give a lecture about it on television. The lecture was such a success that CBS wanted to shift the young reporter to television. At that time, television was new and was not considered a serious form of communication. Walter Cronkite was even more skeptical of television news than of the radio variety. But he thought that if he accepted the television news job, he'd be sent to Korea as a war correspondent. With that adventure in mind, he agreed to the assignment.

But instead of sending him to Korea, CBS put him to work in Washington. Cronkite was furious. "Sold down the river to a lousy local TV station!" he fumed.

But the television assignment turned out to be a fortunate one after all. Cronkite was chosen as anchorman for the 1952 political conventions. There he proved his ability to pick up a microphone on the scene and explain what was happening clearly and accurately. Cronkite's coverage of the national conventions made people see that television was not only a medium of entertainment. They realized that television could make it possible for viewers thousands of miles away to witness history being made.

Suddenly, Walter Cronkite was a star. Besides covering special events, he was asked to do two news shows, "Twentieth Century" and "Eyewitness to History." He became discussion chairman for a program called "Man of the Week." He also

narrated a popular program called "You Are There," in which historical events were reported as if they were happening at the moment.

For the first time in his life, Walter Cronkite was making a great deal of money. Wealth didn't change him. He and Betsy continued to live in their remodeled brownstone house in New York, which was furnished casually and inexpensively. But his $200,000 salary made it possible for Walter to indulge in a few luxuries he hadn't been able to afford before.

Once a check for a lecture was mistakenly mailed directly to him instead of to his business agent. The next morning, instead of taking the train to work, Cronkite stopped off at a used car lot. "What have you got for $1685.90?" he asked. The surprised salesman showed him a second-hand Austin Healey sports car. "I'll take it," said Cronkite, handing over the check. He got in and drove happily off to work.

Rarely did this lighter side of Walter's personality come across on his television programs. He took the news very seriously.

In the mid 1950s, more and more viewers began tuning in the witty new NBC team, Chet Huntley and David Brinkley. NBC started to push ahead of CBS in the ratings.

CBS executives were worried about losing the sponsors for their news programs. They urged Cronkite to adopt a breezier, more light-hearted style. They even made him host of a morning program competing with NBC's *Today* show and hired gag writers to think up jokes for him. But Walter just couldn't bring himself to be funny with the news. CBS ratings continued to drop.

One morning Cronkite read in a TV gossip column that he had been replaced on the morning show by Jack Paar. In the course of the day, he found the rumor was correct.

The 1956 political conventions were an even greater blow.

Four years earlier, everyone had applauded as Walter Cronkite pioneered television coverage of the conventions. But in 1956, the Huntley-Brinkley team stole the show.

In 1960, more viewers were following the Huntley-Brinkley convention coverage. By 1964, competition between the networks had become even more keen. At the Republican Convention that year, reporters and cameramen were everywhere. Walter Cronkite, who was quiet and restrained, got shoved aside.

CBS executives were frantic. They rigged Cronkite with a new headset — one earphone tuned to the speaker's podium and one tuned to the control room. This only added to the confusion. Unable to make sense out of what was happening, Cronkite hesitated and missed cues. "It was as bad a job as I have ever done," he admits.

CBS executives agreed. At the Democratic Convention in 1964, Cronkite was replaced by the team of Roger Mudd and Bob Trout. It was the low point of his career. He was afraid of losing his job.

But CBS news was flooded with mail protesting Cronkite's replacement. The week after the change, the network received 11,000 letters supporting Cronkite. The press also supported him and criticized the network for making the convention coverage a popularity contest.

CBS executives finally realized that to most people, Walter Cronkite is CBS news. They returned him to the anchor spot to cover the November elections. On election night, Cronkite redeemed himself. CBS coverage was excellent.

But it was his superior reporting of the United States space program that finally made Cronkite's position on top secure. When CBS assigned him to head the network's coverage of the Apollo flights, Cronkite spent hundreds of hours finding out about the program. To learn how space equipment operated, he studied instruction manuals and interviewed manufacturers. To find out how it felt to be shot into space, he not only interviewed the astronauts, but also experienced weightlessness himself in a training centrifuge. To be able to describe ground communications accurately, he traveled to all the tracking stations between Florida and Ascension Island in the South Atlantic.

Cronkite communicated all this information to his audience so well that he held people's attention long after each exciting lift-off. During the agonizing hours when the space capsule was out of sight and only garbled messages were coming in from the astronauts, Walter Cronkite's descriptions of what was happening in space kept viewers glued to their television sets.

Hour after hour, Cronkite would remain on camera, hastily snatching a sandwich or a cup of tea during film clips. He didn't sign off until after each successful splash-down in the Pacific Ocean. And then, although he had broadcast for as many as 24 out of 31 straight hours of programming, he seemed to be just getting his second wind.

Besides the space shots, Walter Cronkite has covered most of the major national events of the past 25 years, including the assassinations of President Kennedy and Martin Luther King. He has reported on wars and atomic bomb blasts, riots, crime, over-population, and pollution. Through all kinds of crises, he has remained unruffled, calm, and objective. Only occasionally has he dropped his on-camera reserve.

It happened once in 1962 during the first U.S. manned space flight around the earth. As the rocket carrying John Glenn's space capsule finally lifted off the ground, Cronkite couldn't contain his excitement. "Go, baby, go!" he shouted.

One other time, Walter Cronkite completely forgot himself in front of the cameras. That was the time when President Kennedy was shot. When the news came over the teletype, Cronkite ran into the TV studio in his shirt sleeves and started broadcasting. Tears came into his eyes when he had to announce that the President was dead. He was so shaken he didn't realize until he signed off the air that he'd forgotten to put his suit jacket on.

But Walter Cronkite doesn't often reveal his feelings on the air. He tries hard to be completely objective in reporting the news, whatever his personal feelings or opinions might be. He won't discuss his own politics with interviewers. He won't even comment on the many public officials he's known. He insists that there are very few public figures he doesn't like personally.

Cronkite is afraid the public would think he was prejudiced in editing news stories if he stated his own point of view. He also thinks viewers might be confused if he told them his personal opinion at one point and then switched back to facts. That is a risk he refuses to run. "Some people are better in areas of interpretation," he says. "I think my area is sticking to the facts, the hard news."

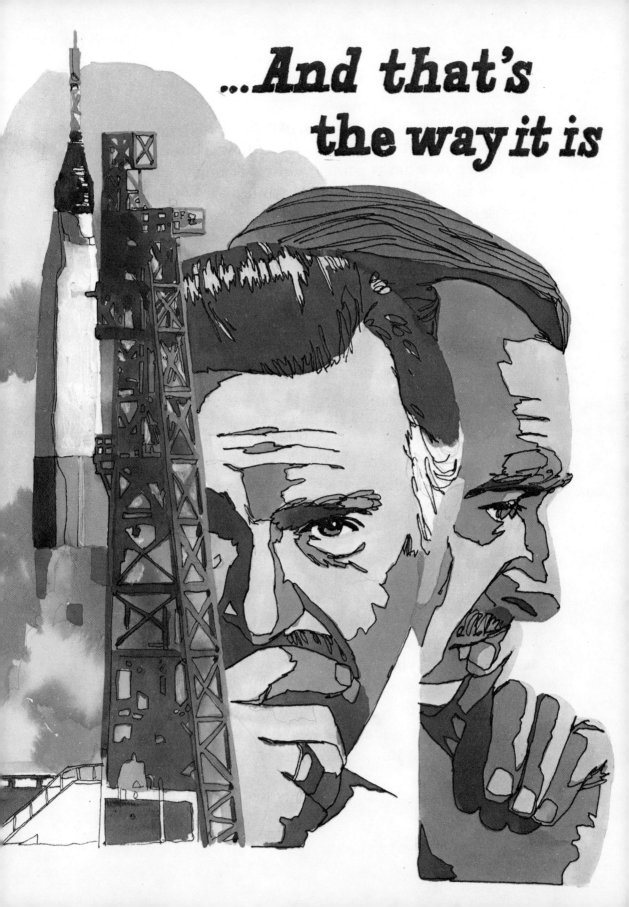

...And that's the way it is

But there is one issue on which Walter Cronkite has consistently been outspoken. He believes the public has a right to know what is going on in government. He feels that people can find out the whole truth only when radio and television, as well as newspapers, are free of government control.

Cronkite is deeply disturbed by the fact that television stations must apply to the government for their licenses to operate. He is afraid that government officials may use their power to force the networks to broadcast a slanted version of the news — to tell only the government's side of the story.

At the 1968 Democratic convention, tight restrictions were placed on the press. A year later, Vice-President Spiro Agnew harshly attacked the networks and threatened them with more government control. It seemed that Walter Cronkite's worst fears were coming true.

Cronkite traveled across the country, speaking out against government control of television. He testified before a Congressional committee. Despite harrassment from Washington, he continued to report criticism of the government.

From the beginning of his career as a newsman, Walter Cronkite has been known for his insistence on presenting both sides of every issue. He has also insisted on getting the facts straight. In fact, he once quit his job rather than broadcast news he hadn't checked out.

On that occasion, Walter was at the microphone at radio station KCMO in Kansas City when the manager dashed in with a hot news item: the new city hall was burning, and two men had just jumped from its roof. Cronkite picked up the phone to check with the fire department, but the station manager stopped him. "Get it on the air," he yelled. "I just got it on the phone from my wife."

Cronkite refused to announce the news without checking it. He quit on the spot and walked out. Later, he had the satisfaction of finding out that the fire was only a small one in a waste basket and that no one had jumped from the roof. In fact, the city hall was still under construction and didn't even have a roof!

Today, Walter Cronkite is just as concerned that the facts he reports are accurate. He rarely gets angry; but when he does, it's likely to be at a staff reporter who has made a careless error or failed to check out the facts. He himself is meticulously careful about checking out even small details.

Some people think Walter Cronkite takes the news a little too seriously. They say he is dull and pompous and that he rarely says anything worth remembering. But his viewers seem to value Cronkite's honesty. Viewers may not recall exactly what he says, but they usually believe it. In a 1973 poll Americans were asked which public figure they trusted the most. Walter Cronkite was the winner, rating far higher than the President, the Vice-President, or any other public official.

Most of his viewers feel they know Walter Cronkite. He has been reporting the news to them for so many years that he seems almost like a member of the family. However, people who know him well say the solemn gentleman who appears on TV isn't the real Walter Cronkite.

Off-camera, Walter is a fun-loving fellow who likes to take his wife Betsy out dancing till the wee hours of the morning. He has a roaring sense of humor and often leaves his friends doubled up with laughter at his hilarious stories and comic imitations.

On the air, Walter Cronkite seems in command of every situation. But off-camera, he is notoriously forgetful. After saying goodby to his family in the morning, he may return home as many as three or four times to retrieve items he's forgotten: his watch, his keys, his briefcase.

Walter loves meeting all kinds of people, but can seldom remember names. Once he talked proudly and at great length to an interviewer about his new-born daughter, "Judy." The reporter later discovered that his daughter's name was Nancy. Judy was the family's cocker spaniel.

Most of Cronkite's TV viewers would never guess that the distinguished-looking newsman who never seems to have a hair out of place is also a race-car enthusiast. For many years Cronkite drove in road rallies and races, including a grueling 12-hour race in Sebring, Florida. Once at an international rally in the Great Smoky Mountains of Tennessee, he was almost killed. The Triumph TR3 he was driving skidded off the road, pitched over an embankment, and tumbled end over end into a river 100 feet below. Walter emerged, soaked, but miraculously unhurt. He had the car fished out of the river and would have finished the race, but the car wouldn't start.

An animal lover, Cronkite once nearly wrecked another car to avoid running over a turtle. Another turtle made its home with the Cronkites for several years. Walter was so fond of it that he even used to take the turtle for walks outside the house. He was genuinely sad when a maid bathed the animal in detergent and brought it to an untimely end.

Unlike some busy fathers, Walter Cronkite is a devoted family man. He has always enjoyed his three children: Nancy, Kathy, and Walter Leland Cronkite, III, who is called Chip. When the children were young, he and Betsy often declined invitations to social events because they preferred staying home. Walter's idea of a good time is to play a game of Monopoly straight through to the end without interruption. He is known as the toughest Monopoly player on East 84th Street.

Cronkite gave up auto racing because he felt it was a selfish sport the family couldn't enjoy with him. Now the Cronkites own a 35-foot sailboat, and the children jokingly refer to their father as "Commodore."

Perhaps because his job requires him to be so objective and matter-of-fact in public life, Walter Cronkite is given to daydreams. He sometimes imagines himself running away to join a circus or sailing a four-masted schooner around the world.

When asked about his plans for retirement, Cronkite muses about owning a small-town newspaper or perhaps going into politics. He says he'd like to see Hong Kong, Oslo, and Addis Ababa. For some reason, he's never managed to get to those cities. But then he smiles wistfully, "Or maybe it might be possible to go to the moon. . . . Can you imagine how great it would be to say to an audience, 'Good evening, ladies and gentlemen. This is Walter Cronkite, reporting for CBS direct from the surface of the moon'?"

Norita Larson

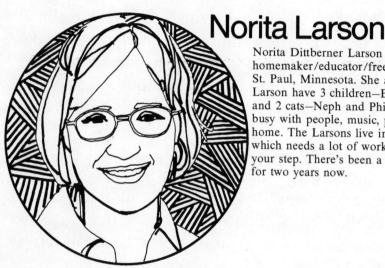

Norita Dittberner Larson is a 30-year old homemaker/educator/free-lance writer living in St. Paul, Minnesota. She and her husband Lee Larson have 3 children—Eric, Jessica and Emily; and 2 cats—Neph and Phineas. Norita's life is busy with people, music, politics, plants, and her home. The Larsons live in a 90-year old home which needs a lot of work, and you have to watch your step. There's been a ladder on the stairway for two years now.

Paula Taylor

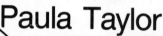

Paula Taylor has only recently begun writing for young people. Having lived in 8 different cities, both in the U. S. and Europe, during the past 10 years, she has held a variety of jobs. She taught writing and literature to junior high school students in Wisconsin and California. In Iceland and the Netherlands, she taught adults basic English. In Athens, Georgia, she was a reader for the blind. A Phi Beta Kappa graduate of Carleton College, her interests range from horticulture to psychic phenomena. Presently, Ms. Taylor lives in Minneapolis, Minnesota with her husband and daughter.

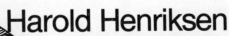

Harold Henriksen

Harold was born in St. Paul, Minnesota and has lived there most of his life. He attended the School of the Associated Arts in St. Paul.

Even while serving in the Army, Harold continued to keep alive his desire to become an artist. In 1965 he was a winner in the All Army Art Contest.

After the Army, Harold returned to Minnesota where he worked for several art studios in the Minneapolis-St. Paul area. In 1967 he became an illustrator for one of the largest art studios in Minneapolis.

During 1971 Harold and his wife traveled to South America where he did on-the-spot drawings for a year. Harold, his wife and daughter Maria now live in Minneapolis where he works as a free lance illustrator.

Walt Disney
Bob Hope
Duke Ellington
Dwight Eisenhower
Coretta King
Pablo Picasso
Ralph Nader
Bill Cosby
Dag Hammarskjold
Sir Frederick Banting

close ups

Mark Twain
Beatrix Potter
Margaret Mead
Rose Kennedy
Walter Cronkite
Henry Kissinger